★ It's My State! ★ ★ ★ ★ ★

TENNESSEE

The Volunteer State

William McGeveran, Rick Petreycik, and Laura L. Sullivan

Cavendish Square

New York

Published in 2016 by Cavendish Square Publishing, LLC
243 5th Avenue, Suite 136, New York, NY 10016

First Edition

Website: cavendishsq.com

This publication represents the opinions and views of the author based on his or her personal experience, knowledge, and research. The information in this book serves as a general guide only. The author and publisher have used their best efforts in preparing this book and disclaim liability rising directly or indirectly from the use and application of this book.

CPSIA Compliance Information: Batch #WS15CSQ

All websites were available and accurate when this book was sent to press.

Library of Congress Cataloging-in-Publication Data

Sullivan, Laura L., 1974-
Tennessee / Laura L. Sullivan, Rick Petreycik, and William McGeveran.
pages cm. — (It's my state!)
Includes bibliographical references and index.
ISBN 978-1-62713-225-1 (hardcover) ISBN 978-1-62713-227-5 (ebook)
1. Tennessee—Juvenile literature. I. Petreycik, Rick. II. McGeveran, William. III. Title.

F436.3.S87 2015
976.8—dc23

2015007191

Editorial Director: David McNamara
Editor: Fletcher Doyle
Copy Editor: Rebecca Rohan
Art Director: Jeffrey Talbot
Designer: Alan Sliwinski
Senior Production Manager: Jennifer Talbot
Production Editor: Renni Johnson
Photo Research: J8 Media

The photographs in this book are used by permission and through the courtesy of: Richard Cummins/Robert Harding World Imagery/Getty Images, cover; Tim Gainey/Alamy, Holly Kuchera/Shutterstock.com, Bartley/All Canada Photos/Superstock, 4; James Urbach/Superstock, Mark A. Schneider/Science Source, Age Fotostock/Superstock, 5; Melinda Fawver/iStock/Thinkstock.com, 6; Jon Bilous/Shutterstock.com, 8; Imagebroker.net/Superstock, 9; Westgraphix LLC, 10; Vernon Siql/Superstock, 12; AgStock Images, Inc./Alamy, 13; Colin1769/File: Belle Meade Plantation.jpg/Wikimedia Commons, Imagebroker.net/Superstock, JoeFox/Alamy, 14; Universal Images Group/Superstock, Thomas R Machnitzki/File: National Civil Rights Museum 4.jpg/ Wikimedia Commons, Lm corle (Own work)/File: Ruby Falls.jpg/Wikimedia Commons, 15; Jamie Adams/Alamy, 16; Age Fotostock/Superstock, 17; Juniors Bildarchiv/Alamy, 19; National Geographic Image Collection/Alamy, Matt Jeppson/Shutterstock.com, Gerard Lacz Images/Superstock, 20; Brian Stansberry/File: Mount-chapman-gsmnp1.jpg /Wikimedia Commons, Nomad/Superstock, Stephen J. Krasemann/Superstock, 21; Nagel Photography/Shutterstock.com, 22; North Wind Pictures Archive/Alamy, 24; North Wind Pictures Archive/Alamy, 25; North Wind Pictures Archive/Alamy, 26; Prisma Bildagentur AG/Alamy, 28; Hulton Archive/Getty Images, 29; Superstock/ Superstock, 32; Everett Collection/Superstock, 33; Bill Cobb/Superstock, Steven Frame/Shutterstock.com, 34; Malcolm MacGregor/Moment/Getty Images, Thomas R Machnitzki (thomas@machnitzki.com) (Own work)/File: Jackson TN downtown Unity Park monument.jpg/Wikimedia Commons, 35; Visual and Written/ Superstock, 36; Print Collector/Hulton Archive/Getty Images, 37; AP Photo/Department of U.S. Army, 38; Photos 12/Alamy, 39; Everett Collection/Superstock, 40; J Steck/iStockphoto.com, 44; Mario Tama/Getty Images, 46; Charley Gallay/Getty Images for Tom Ford, Frederick M. Brown/Getty Images, Chip Somodevilla/ Getty Images, 48; AP Photo, Newberry Library/Superstock, AP Photo/Mark J. Terrill, 49; Ichabod/File: Suggs Creek Cumberland Presbyterian Church Tennessee. jpg/Wikimedia Commons, 52; John Davisson/Invision/AP, Jim West/Age Fotostock/Superstock, 54; Melinda Fawver/Shutterstock.com, AP Photo/Chattanooga Times Free Press, Doug Strickland, 55; Dave Newman/Shutterstock.com, 56; James Kirkikis/Age Fotostock/Superstock, 59; Jim West/Age Fotostock/Superstock, 61; North Wind Picture Archives, Visions of America/Superstock, Evan Agostini/Invision/AP, 62; Mecky/Photographer's Choice/Getty Images, 63; AP Photo/ General Motors, 64; Dennis MacDonald/Alamy, 66; Age Fotostock/Superstock, 67; AgStock Images, Inc./Alamy, Tennessee Valley Authority/File: Great-falls-dam-tva1.jpg/Wikimedia Commons, 68; Age Fotostock/Superstock, AP Photo/John Russell, 69; Vania Georgieva/Shutterstock.com, 70; AP Photo/Mark Humphrey, 73; Christopher Santoro, 74; Epantha/iStock/Thinkstock.com, Travel Bug/Shutterstock.com, 75; Christopher Santoro, 76.

Printed in the United States of America.

TENNESSEE
CONTENTS

A Quick Look at Tennessee 4

1. The Volunteer State 7
Tennessee County Map 10
Tennessee Population by County 11
10 Key Sites 14
10 Key Plants and Animals 20

2. From the Beginning 23
The Native People 26
Making an Eastern Box Turtle 30
10 Key Cities 34
10 Key Dates in State History 43

3. The People 45
10 Key People 48
10 Key Events 54

4. How the Government Works 57
Political Figures from Tennessee 62
You Can Make a Difference 63

5. Making a Living 65
10 Key Industries 68
Recipe for Tennessee Spoon Bread 70

Tennessee State Map 74
Tennessee Map Skills 75
State Flag, Seal, and Song 76
Glossary 77
More About Tennessee 78
Index 79

★ State Tree: Tulip Poplar

Many of Tennessee's early settlers made their houses, barns, and places of business out of tulip poplar wood. The tree has smooth, brownish-gray bark and flowers that look like green-orange tulips. The tulip poplar was made the state tree in 1947.

★ State Wild Animal: Raccoon

In 1971, the Tennessee legislature adopted the raccoon as the state wild animal. This mammal, about the size of a large cat, has black mask markings on its face and a long striped tail. Raccoons eat berries, nuts, insects, small birds and their eggs, frogs, and fish, or steal food from garbage cans.

★ State Bird: Mockingbird

The grayish-white mockingbird makes its home throughout Tennessee. Known for its beautiful singing voice, the mockingbird also imitates, or mocks, the songs of other birds. That is how it got its name. The mockingbird became Tennessee's state bird in 1933.

TENNESSEE

★ State Wildflower: Passionflower

The passionflower, which comes in varying shades of purple, blue, and white, has several different names. People call it a maypop, a wild apricot, or an ocoee. In 1973, the state legislature agreed to make the passionflower the state wildflower and the iris the state cultivated flower.

★ State Fossil: *Pterotrigonia (Scabrotrigonia) thoracica*

The bivalve shell Pterotrigonia (Scabrotrigonia) thoracica was named the state fossil in 1998. Like the oyster and the clam, it has two shells that hinge together. These creatures lived more than seventy million years ago in an ocean that once covered what is now West Tennessee. The "spokes-fossil" is nicknamed "Ptero."

★ State Insects: Firefly and Ladybug

In 1975, the Tennessee legislature named two state insects: the firefly and the ladybug. The firefly gives off a glow-in-the-dark light that makes it easy to spot on summer evenings. Ladybugs, with their spotted red wings, also stand out. They feed on the insects that harm crops.

The Tennessee River meanders
around Chattanooga and through
the Cumberland Plateau.

The Volunteer State

Tennessee has forests, mountains, valleys, and rolling rivers. It lies in a region of the United States that is commonly called the Upper South, which is distinct from the Lower South, or the Deep South. Other states often considered part of the Upper South include Virginia, North Carolina, Arkansas, and Kentucky.

The state has a shape similar to a huge rectangle. It stretches about 440 miles (710 kilometers) from the Mississippi River on the west to the Appalachian Mountains on the east and extends 120 miles (190 km) from north to south. With a land area of 41,235 square miles (106,798 square kilometers), Tennessee ranks thirty-fourth in size among the fifty states.

Tennessee is divided into ninety-five counties. The biggest, in both area and population, is Shelby County, in the southwest corner. Memphis, the state's largest city, is located in this county. Memphis is also the largest city located on the Mississippi River, as well as the third largest city in the southeastern United States and the twentieth largest city in the entire United States.

The state of Tennessee can also be divided into three broad regions of roughly equal size. These geographic, and cultural, areas are East Tennessee, Middle Tennessee, and West Tennessee. They are known as Tennessee's "grand divisions."

The fog, or mist, that collects at higher altitudes gives the Great Smoky Mountains their name.

East Tennessee

East Tennessee is a rugged region with many high mountain peaks. The Blue Ridge Mountains, part of the Appalachian mountain chain, are spread along Tennessee's eastern border. The mountain ranges in Tennessee include the Unaka mountain range and the Great Smoky Mountains. The Smokies, home of Great Smoky Mountains National Park, got their name from the bluish-gray haze that often hovers around their peaks. This isn't actually smoke, but fog or mist caused by humid air from the Gulf of Mexico rapidly cooling as it hits the cold, high mountains. The name Unaka, from a Cherokee word meaning "white," also commonly refers to all the mountains along Tennessee's eastern border with North Carolina.

The highest section of the Smokies is within Great Smoky Mountains National Park. Part of the park is in Tennessee, and the rest is in North Carolina. Clingmans Dome lies inside the park.

Tennessee Borders

North:	Kentucky Virginia
South:	Mississippi Alabama Georgia
East:	North Carolina
West:	Arkansas Missouri

At 6,643 feet (2,025 meters), it is Tennessee's highest peak and the third-highest peak in the United States east of the Mississippi River. Clingmans Dome has a 45-foot (13.7 m) observation tower that allows for a **panoramic** view of the nearby scenery and mountain ranges. The trail leading to the mountaintop is a favorite of hikers.

The area to the west of the Blue Ridge Mountains is part of the Great Appalachian Valley, or Great Valley. This section of East Tennessee is a high, **fertile**, wooded area with flat-topped mountains that range in height from 1,500 to 1,800 feet (457 to 549 m). The upper Tennessee River flows south through the area, and there are many streams and wide valleys. Knoxville, Tennessee's third-largest city, is located on the upper Tennessee River. It served as Tennessee's first capital. Knoxville is one of the gateways to Great Smoky Mountains National Park and is known for cherishing and promoting Appalachian culture.

In Their Own Words

"It is good and right that we should conserve these mountain heights of the old frontier for the benefit of the American people."
—President Franklin Delano Roosevelt, dedicating Great Smoky Mountains National Park in 1940

The rushing waters of the Ocoee River in eastern Tennessee provide opportunities for recreation.

TENNESSEE
COUNTY MAP

TENNESSEE
POPULATION BY COUNTY

Anderson 75,129	Hamilton 336,463	Morgan 21,987
Bedford 45,058	Hancock 6,819	Obion 31,807
Benton 16,489	Hardeman 27,253	Overton 22,083
Bledsoe 12,876	Hardin 26,026	Perry 7,915
Blount 123,010	Hawkins 56,833	Pickett 5,077
Bradley 98,963	Haywood 18,787	Polk 16,825
Campbell 40,716	Henderson 27,769	Putnam 72,321
Cannon 13,801	Henry 32,330	Rhea 31,809
Carroll 28,522	Hickman 24,690	Roane 54,181
Carter 57,424	Houston 8,426	Robertson 66,283
Cheatham 39,105	Humphreys 18,538	Rutherford 262,604
Chester 17,131	Jackson 11,638	Scott 22,228
Claiborne 32,213	Jefferson 51,407	Sequatchie 14,112
Clay 7,861	Johnson 18,244	Sevier 89,889
Cocke 35,662	Knox 432,226	Shelby 927,644
Coffee 52,796	Lake 7,832	Smith 19,166
Crockett 14,586	Lauderdale 27,815	Stewart 13,324
Cumberland 56,053	Lawrence 41,869	Sullivan 156,823
Davidson 626,681	Lewis 12,161	Sumner 160,645
Decatur 11,757	Lincoln 33,361	Tipton 61,081
Dekalb 18,723	Loudon 48,556	Trousdale 7,870
Dickson 49,666	McMinn 52,266	Unicoi 18,313
Dyer 38,335	McNairy 26,075	Union 19,109
Fayette 38,412	Macon 22,248	Van Buren 5,548
Fentress 17,959	Madison 98,294	Warren 39,839
Franklin 41,052	Marion 28,237	Washington 122,979
Gibson 49,683	Marshall 30,617	Wayne 17,021
Giles 29,485	Maury 80,956	Weakley 35,021
Grainger 22,657	Meigs 11,753	White 25,841
Greene 68,831	Monroe 44,519	Williamson 202,686
Grundy 13,703	Montgomery 172,331	Wilson 113,993
Hamblen 62,544	Moore 6,362	

Source: US Bureau of the Census, 2010

To the west of the Great Appalachian Valley is the Cumberland Plateau, which also extends beyond the state to the north and south. (A plateau is an area of high, relatively flat land, or tableland.) It is a fairly rugged region, with the flat land often broken up by deep, narrow valleys. Chattanooga, which is Tennessee's fourth-largest city, is located on the Cumberland Plateau in the tri-state border region, where Tennessee, Georgia, and Alabama meet.

Middle Tennessee

Middle Tennessee's natural landscape is shaped like a deep bowl. The outer edge of this bowl, called the Highland Rim, has steep mountain slopes made mostly of a kind of rock called **limestone**. Limestone is a sedimentary rock that is generally formed by the remains of marine life. Much of Tennessee was once under a shallow sea. Beneath the surface of the rim are a number of hollowed out caves and underground streams. The limestone bedrock in the area has been worn away by fresh water, leading to the cave systems.

The area inside the bowl is known as the Nashville Basin. Covering more than 6,450 square miles (16,700 sq km), this mostly flat region has some of the richest farmland in the state. Crops grown here include wheat, potatoes, tomatoes, tobacco, and various types of fruit. Because of the soil's high concentration of limestone, which contains many nutrients, the Nashville Basin is also perfect pastureland. Grasses grow well there and are the ideal fodder for many different kinds of livestock. As a result, beef and dairy cattle, sheep, and horses have been raised in Middle Tennessee.

The pastures of middle Tennessee are ideal for raising horses and other livestock.

Soybeans are the largest crop in Tennessee.

Winding some 280 miles (450 km) through Middle Tennessee is the scenic Duck River. This is the longest river that flows entirely within Tennessee, without going into any other state. A huge variety of freshwater fish, shellfish, and other marine life live in the Duck River. It has one of the largest varieties of living things in its waters of all the rivers in North America.

Middle Tennessee's major cities include Clarksville, Murfreesboro, and Nashville, which is Tennessee's capital and second-largest city. Clarksville and Nashville are both located along the Cumberland River, which loops through the northern part of Middle Tennessee.

West Tennessee

West Tennessee is made up of low, fertile flatlands occasionally broken up by hills, valleys, and streams. This region, sometimes called the Jackson Plain, is part of the nation's Upper East Gulf Coastal Plain. It lies between two big rivers. On the western side of West Tennessee is the flood plain of the Mississippi, which flows along the state's border. On the eastern side of this region is the Tennessee River. That river starts out in East Tennessee, where it flows south into northern Alabama. It crosses that state from east to west and then loops back up to go through West Tennessee, this time flowing north.

Tennessee's far western edge has some of the best farmland in the state. That is because the Mississippi River, which forms Tennessee's western border, carries silt—a rich collection of sand, clay, and other minerals—and deposits it along the surrounding banks. These minerals enrich the soil, allowing crops to be grown more easily. Cotton and soybeans are two of the major crops that grow in the nutrient-rich soil. Trees that flourish

10 KEY SITES ★ ★ ★

Belle Meade Plantation

Dollywood

Graceland

1. Belle Meade Plantation

This historic **plantation** mansion in Nashville is a museum. The 30-acre (12.1-hectare) site features many original buildings, as well as reconstructed slave quarters, to show what life was like in Tennessee in the nineteenth century. There is also a winery.

2. Country Music Hall of Fame and Museum

The Country Music Hall of Fame and Museum in downtown Nashville preserves the history of country music while educating the public about the genre. The museum collections exhibit two centuries of country music history, while the hall honors its stars.

3. Creative Discovery Museum

Located in downtown Chattanooga near the riverfront, this museum hopes to "inspire all children to explore, innovate, create, and play." It has interactive exhibits, knowledgeable staff, and a science theater for performing chemistry and physics experiments.

4. Dollywood

Owned by music legend Dolly Parton and located in Pigeon Forge, Dollywood theme park is the biggest ticketed attraction in Tennessee. It has thrill rides, country crafts, and musical events. Closed in the winter, it still attracts about three million guests each year.

5. Graceland

Graceland, in Memphis, was once the private home of music icon Elvis Presley. After his death, it was made into a museum. It is one of the most visited private homes in the United States. Its famous front gate looks like a book of sheet music.

6. Great Smoky Mountains National Park

This park is partly in Tennessee, partly in North Carolina. At 522,419 acres (211,415 ha), it is one of the largest natural preserves in the country. It has hiking trails, visitor centers, and historic sites such as Cades Cove, a valley with preserved log cabins and barns.

7. Memphis Zoo

Located in midtown Memphis, the Memphis Zoo has more than five hundred species of animals, and more than 3,500 animals in total. Its exhibits include Animals of the Night, the Zambezi River Hippo Camp, and Cat Country.

8. Mud Island

Mud Island is a celebration of all things relating to the Mississippi River. This peninsula (not really an island) is located in Memphis and includes the Mud Island River Park, the Mississippi River Museum, and the Mud Island Amphitheatre.

9. National Civil Rights Museum

This complex of historic sites and museums in Memphis traces the history of **civil rights** in the United States. The primary site is built around the Lorraine Hotel, where civil rights hero Martin Luther King Jr. was shot and killed.

10. Ruby Falls

The spectacular Ruby Falls is located inside of Lookout Mountain, which straddles Alabama, Georgia, and Tennessee. Ruby Falls is located near Chattanooga. Visitors can tour the Ruby Falls Cave and watch the waterfall cascade inside the mountain.

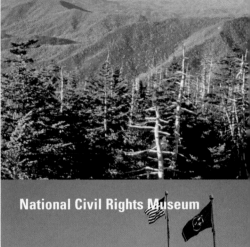

Great Smoky Mountains National Park

National Civil Rights Museum

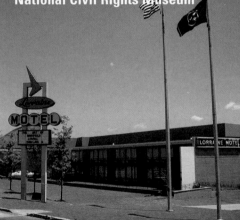

Ruby Falls

Parking lots around LP Field and other areas of Nashville were flooded in the spring of 2010 when the Cumberland River overflowed its banks.

in this region are used for timber. Flooding can be a problem for residents who live near the river. In the great Mississippi floods of 2011, for example, more than 1,300 homes in Memphis had to be evacuated due to dangerous flood waters.

Memphis, which is on the Mississippi River, is a center of cotton trading and hardwood manufacturing. It is the home of the music style known as the blues and can make a claim as the birthplace of rock 'n' roll. Graceland, the former home of legendary singer Elvis Presley, is located in Memphis. It is now a museum to his memory and attracts more than six hundred thousand visitors every year.

Climate

Most of Tennessee is classified as having a humid, subtropical climate. The state tends to have hot, wet summers. In Memphis, July temperatures average around 83 degrees Fahrenheit (28 degrees Celsius), with daily highs averaging 92°F (33°C). As in many places in the South, high humidity levels can make the temperature feel much hotter. In Nashville, July temperatures average around 79°F (26°C). Higher areas, such as the Cumberland Plateau and

The Volunteer State

Tennessee's nickname is the **Volunteer** State. It got that name during the War of 1812, a conflict between the United States and Great Britain and its North American colonies and Native American allies. Tennessee's volunteer soldiers played a big role in that war, particularly at the Battle of New Orleans.

the mountains of the east, are cooler. Parts of the Appalachians are considered to have a mountain temperate climate.

Winters in Tennessee are generally mild. January temperatures in Nashville and Memphis average 38°F (3°C), and daily lows are around 30°F (–1°C). Snowfall can be heavy in the mountains of East Tennessee, but most of the state gets little snow. The state's average annual precipitation, which includes rain, snow, and sleet, is around 50 inches (125 centimeters), but it varies by region.

Despite a mild climate, Tennessee has experienced some extreme weather conditions. The state's lowest temperature occurred in Mountain View on December 30, 1917, when the mercury dropped to a numbing –32°F (–36°C). A record high was hit during 1930 in Perryville, when temperatures soared to 113°F (45°C) on both July 29 and August 9.

For most of the state, the greatest precipitation occurs in winter and spring. Heavy rains in the winter of 1937 caused rivers to overflow, leaving many people dead, injured, or homeless. It was the worst flooding in Tennessee history. The Tennessee Valley Authority, starting in the late 1930s, has built many **dams** that have helped control floodwaters over the years, but flooding can still be severe. In 2010, the Cumberland River flooded the Nashville area, killing twenty-six people. A year later, the Mississippi crested at near-record heights in Memphis and flooded parts of the city and surrounding areas.

Bobcats live in limited numbers in eastern Tennessee.

Tornadoes are common in Tennessee. Tennesseans brace themselves for tornado season, from March through August. Forecasters today can tell when a tornado is forming in a certain area, so people sometimes have time to take cover. But these storms can still be deadly. From April 25 to 28, 2011, about three hundred tornadoes hit seven Southern states. It was the worst single outbreak of tornadoes ever recorded in the United States. Although Alabama was the hardest hit, more than thirty people were killed in Tennessee.

Tennessee ranks second in the number of tornado deaths nationwide, after Florida. Though tornadoes are more common in states like Oklahoma and Kansas, they tend to be more deadly in the Southeast. There are more mobile homes, which are especially vulnerable to tornadoes. They also tend to strike at night, so people aren't as likely to receive warnings, and also descend from lower clouds, making them harder to see, particularly amid trees and buildings.

Wildlife

When it comes to the outdoors, Tennessee is a natural paradise. Half of the state is covered in forests, which are home to at least 150 different kinds of native trees. Evergreen trees such as hemlock, spruce, white pine, and southern balsam thrive in East Tennessee, along with hardwood trees such as maple, cherry, yellow poplar, and oak. In Middle Tennessee, red cedars populate the Highland Rim, while sweet gum, sycamore, and scrub oak can be found within the Nashville Basin. Bald cypress, cottonwood, tupelo gum, water oak, pecan, swamp locust, and catalpa trees grow in the fertile soil of West Tennessee.

A unique tree feature is the Southern Appalachian spruce-fir forest that covers Clingmans Dome. Red spruce and Fraser fir flourish on this, the highest point in Tennessee (and the highest peak of the Appalachian Mountain range). This kind of **ecosystem** can survive only at the highest, coldest elevations. The spruce-fir forest is a relic of the last Ice Age and is sometimes called a Canadian or boreal forest, for its resemblance to the forests in the extreme north of North America. This area is home to several endangered and threatened species. The forest was heavily damaged by logging in the past. More recently, many Fraser firs have been killed by an invasive, non-native insect.

Many types of wildflowers brighten Tennessee's woods and fields. These include passionflowers, dragonroot, hop clovers, azaleas, holly, mountain laurels, and rhododendrons. Every spring, many wildflower enthusiasts visit Tennessee to view the new blooms. Some of the wildflowers are under threat. Habitat loss has reduced the numbers of some once common species. Some plant and flower species are even poached, or illegally taken by collectors. Trillium species, with their three petals in a variety of colors, are often stolen for private gardens. Some thieves also steal rare orchids.

Golden Eagles

Though golden eagles are primarily western birds, they are winter visitors to Tennessee. It is thought that they once nested in Tennessee, but they no longer do. However, researchers have found that their numbers have slightly increased in Tennessee.

The illegal harvesting of the plant ginseng, which is thought to have medicinal qualities, has become more commonplace. Rangers do their best to stop the poachers, but with ginseng roots being sold for up to $900 a pound, many criminals are still illegally taking the plants.

Tennessee is home to fifty-one mammal species, from huge black bears to the tiny pygmy shrew. Mammal species in Tennessee's woods include deer, rabbits, raccoons, skunks, beavers, muskrats, bobcats, flying squirrels, and red and gray foxes. In mountainous areas, you can even find European wild boar, also known as razorbacks. It is believed that the first of these entered the Tennessee wild in 1920 after escaping from a game preserve in North Carolina. **Feral** pigs, or those descended from domestic animals, are a nuisance in some parts of Tennessee.

European wild boars cause a lot of damage to crops.

Among the birds that nest in Tennessee, or pass through the state on their migration route, are mockingbirds, cardinals, robins, eastern bluebirds, wood thrushes, eastern towhees, and Carolina wrens. Egrets and herons nest along rivers and streams. Game birds such as ducks, geese, and quails are nearly everywhere, too. Wild turkeys can be spotted in remote parts of the eastern mountains.

Many kinds of fish make their home in Tennessee's rivers, lakes, and streams. These include trout, walleye, bluegills, bream, catfish, and bass. The channel, or fiddler, catfish, Tennessee's most common catfish, was named the state commercial fish in 1988. The smallmouth bass got the title of state sport fish in 2005. A few types of fish, such as the bluemask darter and pallid sturgeon, are listed by the federal government as endangered.

Other endangered species include the Indiana bat, Carolina northern flying squirrel, least tern, and spruce-fir moss spider. Endangered whooping cranes are not native to Tennessee and do not nest there. But some stop off in the state each year on their way south.

Black Bear

Cave Salamander

Eastern Box Turtle

1. Black Bear

Black bears can weigh as much as 500 pounds (227 kilograms), though the average is less than 200 pounds (91 kg). They live in many of Tennessee's forests. Black bears are omnivores, meaning they eat nuts and berries as well as meat.

2. Cave Salamander

Named the state amphibian in 1995, the cave salamander lives in streams within limestone caves. It is 4 to 8 inches (10 to 20 centimeters) long and has feathery red gills. Cave salamanders are threatened in Tennessee due to pollution.

3. Eastern Box Turtle

Chosen as the state reptile in 1995, the eastern box turtle is usually less than 6 inches (15 cm) long. These land turtles are slow to mature but may live for one hundred years. They eat insects, berries, mushrooms, and worms.

4. Eastern Spotted Skunk

The eastern spotted skunk has four wavy white lines on black fur, giving it a spotted or blotchy appearance. When they see danger, they will stamp their feet in warning, do a handstand, and launch their bad-smelling spray.

5. Elk

Elk, or red deer, were once abundant in Tennessee but were hunted to extinction there. However, they survived in other places and have been reintroduced to Tennessee forests. Elk can weigh up to 1,100 pounds (499 kg).

6. Fraser Fir

The Fraser fir, the most popular Christmas tree in the United States, grows to a maximum of 80 feet (24.4 m) and lives at high elevations. This tree is threatened by a small, non-native insect called the balsam woolly adelgid, but it is widely cultivated on tree farms.

Fraser Fir

7. Mountain Laurel

The mountain laurel has pink and white flowers and shiny, dark green leaves. It grows to a height of 10 to 30 feet (3 to 9 m), and thrives in the mountains and on rocky slopes. Mountain laurels are poisonous to most animals.

8. Robin

The robin came in a close second, behind the mockingbird, in voting for the state bird in 1933. Robins live year-round in Tennessee and are a common sight. Noted for their cheery song and bright orange breast, they eat berries and worms.

9. Tennessee Purple Coneflower

The Tennessee purple coneflower has striking purple petals and grows to about 30 inches (76.2 cm) tall. This plant, rescued from the endangered list by conservation efforts, is found in only three counties in central Tennessee.

Mountain Laurel

10. Woodchuck

The woodchuck, also known as a groundhog or whistle-pig, is a large type of ground squirrel that can grow to a length of 2 feet (.6 m). Woodchucks dig underground homes, called burrows, and eat grasses and many types of agricultural crops.

Woodchuck

The John Oliver Place in Cades Cove is one of many historic buildings in Eastern Tennessee.

From the Beginning

Archaeologists—scientists who study the remains of past cultures—estimate that humans first entered what is now Tennessee more than twelve thousand years ago, toward the end of the last Ice Age. These people, known as Paleo-Indians, moved from place to place in small groups, hunting large animals such as mastodons, giant armadillos, and sabre-toothed tigers. Some of the caves along riverbanks reveal blackened, charred walls where these people built fires and cooked meals.

Scientists believe that by about 8000 BCE, the climate had warmed. The big animals died out from a combination of climate change and hunting. The people survived by fishing, hunting small game, and gathering plants to eat.

By around 1000 BCE, what scientists call the Woodland culture had developed. The Woodland culture peoples, which included several tribes, learned to plant corn and other crops and developed new tools, such as the bow and arrow. They also built large mounds, which historians believe were used mostly as burial grounds.

Around 1000 CE, a more advanced culture developed, known as Mississippian because it was centered in the Mississippi Valley. Mississippian peoples, or tribes, relied on farming, stored food for winter, and made jewelry and other ornaments. They settled in large fortified towns ruled by chiefs and built mounds for burial or religious worship. By the time Europeans arrived in the 1500s, these villages had mostly disappeared.

Three other groups, however, had settled in the region—the Cherokee, the Creek, and the Chickasaw. These Native Americans lived in villages and planted squash, corn, and beans. They also gathered nuts and berries, fished, and hunted deer and turkey. In winter, several families shared a large rectangular house made of logs. During the summer, people lived in houses made of tree branches woven together and plastered with mud.

Europeans Arrive

Spanish explorer Hernando de Soto led the first group of Europeans to enter the region. De Soto and his men were looking for gold, which they never found. During their travels, in 1540 and 1541, they mistreated the Native Americans they encountered. They also spread germs against which the Native Americans had no immunity. Diseases such as smallpox, measles, and diphtheria spread from village to village, killing many Native Americans.

More than a century later, in 1673, Englishmen James Needham and Gabriel Arthur entered the area hoping to start a fur trade. They were taken prisoner by the Cherokee, and Needham was killed. But Arthur lived with the Cherokee people for a time and even fought with them in battle. He was allowed to return to the colony of North Carolina, where he told people about forests filled with beavers, mink, and otters. The pelts, or fur, of these animals could be turned into coats and other valuable goods. Within a year, English colonists were crossing the mountains to hunt in the land that would become Tennessee.

The early Native population hunted large mammals such as the mastodon.

Spanish explorer Hernando de Soto was seeking gold when he led his men into what is now Tennessee.

France also began to turn its eyes toward this area. In 1682, the French explorer René-Robert Cavelier, sieur de La Salle (often called La Salle), claimed the Mississippi Valley for France. Thirty-two years later, in 1714, a French officer and trader named Charles Charleville established a trading post at French Lick, near present-day Nashville. By the early 1750s, Great Britain and France were competing for control of the fur trade with the region's Native Americans.

In Europe, the French and the British had been waging war against each other for decades, and that conflict spilled over into North America. The French and Indian War, which broke out in 1754, involved France and Great Britain, along with Native American groups allied with one side or the other. In 1763, the war came to a close, and Great Britain, the victor, gained almost all of France's land east of the Mississippi River. While under British rule, the land that includes present-day Tennessee became part of the colony of North Carolina.

Early Settlers

After the French and Indian War, pioneers from coastal areas started settling in the region. In 1769, North Carolinians established a settlement along the Watauga and Nolichucky Rivers. In 1772, they established a system of self-government called the Watauga Association. When the British colonial governor of North Carolina found out about the Watauga Association, he was not pleased, but he left it alone.

Around the same time, a North Carolinian named Richard Henderson took an interest in the area. He was a land speculator, which meant that he bought land in order to sell it at a higher price. Henderson hired a skilled woodsman named Daniel Boone to cut a trail from Virginia through the Cumberland Mountains into Kentucky. The trail—called the Wilderness Road—became the main route into Tennessee.

The Native People

Around twelve thousand years ago, people lived in the area that is now Tennessee. They hunted mastodons and other huge animals that lived during that time, using spear heads made of flint. Later, a group known as the Mound Builders lived in the area and elsewhere in the Southeast. Around the time the earliest settlers arrived, the tribes living in Tennessee included the Cherokee, Chickasaw, Creek, Koasati, Quapaw, Shawnee, and Yuchi tribes.

The tribes survived with a combination of hunting (for deer, elk, rabbits, turkeys, etc.) and farming. The men mostly hunted, while the women tended the crops, which included maize, beans, and squash. They also gathered wild plants. The tribes wore clothes made of either leather or woven fibers. Though most wore a covering on the bottom—breechclout and leggings for men, a wraparound skirt for women—they often didn't wear clothing on top. The tribes mostly lived in settled villages. One of the largest, the Cherokee town of Tanasi, gave the state of Tennessee its name.

The Chucalissa Archaeological Site near Memphis contains exhibits on life in the Mississippian Culture.

Native American relations with European explorers and settlers were mixed. In the 1550s, Spanish explorers allied with one of the Creek tribes to help them fight an enemy tribe. Later, though, local tribes destroyed all Spanish settlements in the area. Europeans brought several diseases, including smallpox, to which the Native Americans had no resistance. As a result, a large percentage of the First People of Tennessee died not long after European contact. Later, in 1838 and 1839, the US government forced the tribes remaining in Tennessee to relocate. By then, mainly the Cherokee remained. Around seventeen thousand

Cherokee were ordered to walk from Tennessee to the new Indian Territory established west of Arkansas. More than four thousand of Tennessee's Cherokee died along what is now known as the Trail of Tears.

Today, there are no federally recognized Native American tribes in Tennessee. The descendants of the tribes removed in the 1800s now live on reservations in Oklahoma. There are, however, some Native American groups in Tennessee who preserve their heritage but are not federally recognized. These include the Chikamaka Cherokee and the Etowah Cherokee Nation.

Spotlight on the Cherokee

Cherokee is pronounced "CHAIR-uh-kee." The name is from a Muskogee word that means "speakers of another language" but the tribe originally called itself "Aniyunwiya" which means "the real or principal people."

Men's Roles: Historically, aspects of daily life were divided between the genders. Men usually did all of the hunting, and if there was a conflict with another tribe they were the ones who did all of the fighting. They were also in charge of diplomatic negotiations with other tribes, and politics within their own tribe. Men were the tribal chiefs.

Women's Roles: In Cherokee history, women were in charge of many things. They were allowed to own property, and they were in charge of the land. Women tended the fields and made decisions about agriculture. They also made social and family decisions, regarding such things as marriage. Clan relationships were traced through the mothers, not the fathers. Both men and women were storytellers, artists, and healers.

Homes and Villages: Cherokees liked to make their homes near a river, so they would have a source of water and fish, and also a means of travel in dugout canoes. Houses were made with cane and plaster walls and thatched roofs. Larger ceremonial buildings had seven sides. Most villages also had a ball field, with a place for spectators.

Cherokee Art: When they lived in Tennessee and other areas of the Southeast, the Cherokee were known for their pottery, gourd art, reed baskets, and carved pipes. When they were forcibly relocated to reservations out west they could no longer get the materials they needed, so they turned to other arts such as beading and making textiles such as rugs and blankets.

The Wilderness Road into eastern Tennessee passed through the Cumberland Gap.

Once the trail was cut, Henderson wanted to gain control of the land around it. So in 1775, he struck a deal with local Cherokee leaders at a place called Sycamore Shoals. In exchange for guns, ammunition, and other goods, the Cherokee gave Henderson and his Transylvania Land Company more than 20 million acres (8 million hectares) of land in what are now Tennessee and Kentucky. But many Cherokee believed they had been swindled and continued to attack settlements for a time.

In Their Own Words

"Fame is like a shaved pig with a greased tail, and it is only after it has slipped through the hands of some thousands, that some fellow, by mere chance, holds onto it!"
—Frontiersman, politician, folk hero, and Tennessee resident Davy Crockett

In 1779, Henderson sold a huge tract of land around the Cumberland River to a group of adventurous pioneers. They erected a fort on the banks of the river, naming it Fort Nashborough. A few years later the settlement's name was changed to Nashville.

Spirit of Independence

The settlers of European descent in what is now Tennessee mostly welcomed the American Revolution (1775–1783). Though they lived far from most of the fighting, when they found out that the British planned to take control of their territory, they sprang into action.

In September 1780, volunteers from the area called the Overmountain Men joined forces with men from today's North Carolina and Virginia at Sycamore Shoals. The group set out on a long journey to track down Major Patrick Ferguson, the British military leader in charge of controlling their region. The troops, under the leadership of Colonel John Sevier of Watauga, caught up with Ferguson and his forces at Kings Mountain in South Carolina. Firing their muskets from behind trees and bushes, they defeated the British after only an hour of fighting.

The war ended in 1783. Great Britain recognized American independence. North Carolina—including its western territory from the Appalachian Mountains to the Mississippi River—now became part of the new nation known as the United States of America.

The settlers in this remote region still had to deal with the threat of Native American attacks. The North Carolina legislature was not willing to provide aid, so the settlers felt they were on their own. Representatives from three counties met in Jonesboro and, after much debate, drafted a constitution for a "separate and distinct state." They named it Franklin, in honor of the American patriot Benjamin Franklin, and at a later meeting, they elected Colonel Sevier—hero of the Battle of Kings Mountain—as governor.

The settlers tried unsuccessfully to get Franklin admitted to the United States as a separate state, while a smaller group sided with the North Carolina government. Disputes with the Cherokee over land claims also led to open warfare between settlers and Native

John Sevier was the first governor of Tennessee.

Americans. The "state" of Franklin fell apart after only a few years, and North Carolina offered the territory to the federal government. The government accepted, creating a new Southwest Territory, with Knoxville as its capital.

Other territories bordering the original thirteen colonies were now becoming states. In January 1796, the people of the Southwest Territory requested statehood for themselves. On June 1, 1796, Tennessee officially became the sixteenth US state, with John Sevier as its first governor.

Making an Eastern Box Turtle

The Eastern Box Turtle was chosen as the state reptile of Tennessee in 1995. These turtles can live to be one hundred years old! Follow the instructions below to make your own box turtle.

What You Need

Paper bowl

Plastic spoon

Green and yellow construction paper

Safety scissors

Pencil

Green and brown markers

Two googly eyes

Pencil

Glue

What to Do

- Cut out twenty to twenty-five octagonal shapes from green construction paper and glue them to the outside of the paper bowl. The bowl should be turned upside-down with the opening facing the table.

- Use the brown marker to color in the space left around the octagonal shapes.

- Rip up small pieces of yellow construction paper, and glue some of them to each of the octagonal shapes.

- Use a pencil to draw the outline of the turtle's four legs and tail, and cut them out with the safety scissors.

- Glue the legs and tail to the underside of the rim of the bowl.

- Use the green marker to color the back of the plastic spoon green, and glue the googly eyes to the bottom side of the round part of the spoon.

- Use the safety scissors to poke a hole in the side of the bowl opposite the tail. Insert the handle of the plastic spoon into the hole (googly eyes facing up) and secure it with glue.

A New State

More and more settlers poured into the area through the Wilderness Road, seeking new opportunities. To make room for them, the federal government in 1818 purchased from the Chickasaw a large piece of land, stretching to the Mississippi River in the west. In 1819, a port town was established on the Mississippi, and the settlers named it Memphis.

Although there was some industry, especially ironworks, farming remained the main source of income for Tennesseans. The state set money aside to develop roads and bridges. By 1820, more than four hundred thousand people were living in Tennessee. By 1850, there were more than a million Tennesseans.

Capital for a Day

Kingston was Tennessee's capital for one day, September 21, 1807. The Cherokee agreed to give up land if Kingston would be the new state capital. The Tennessee General Assembly tricked the Cherokee, upholding its end of the deal by meeting in Kingston that day, then moving the capital back to Knoxville.

In 1829, a Tennessean named Andrew Jackson became president of the United States. He had served in the US Congress and was a widely admired military leader from the War of 1812. By the time he ran for the presidency in 1828 he was a wealthy landowner, but he campaigned as a champion of the common man.

Jackson did help ordinary settlers in Tennessee, but it was at the expense of the Native Americans who were living there. In 1830, Congress, at Jackson's insistence, passed the Indian Removal Act. The act called for the Cherokee people to be removed from their land in Tennessee and other southeastern states to an area west of the Mississippi River. In this way, Cherokee land would become available to white settlers.

In 1838, federal troops rounded up thousands of Cherokee men, women, and children and forced them to march more than 1,200 miles (2,000 km) to a barren, deserted section of present-day Oklahoma. With hardly any food or medical supplies and no warm clothes to protect them from winter weather, many died of hunger or disease on the way. Their terrible journey became known as the Trail of Tears.

Slavery and the Civil War

By the early to mid-1800s, **slavery** was becoming a big issue in the country. Many white people in the Deep South felt slavery was vital to their economy. Without slave labor,

The Hermitage Mansion, built by future president Andrew Jackson on his plantation, was completed in 1819.

In Their Own Words

"And yet there's no sound reason why women, if they have the time and ability, shouldn't sit with men on city councils, in state legislatures, or in the House or Senate."
—Senator Hattie Wyatt Caraway, born and raised in Tennessee [served as senator for Arkansas]

they would struggle to run their large farms, or plantations. They also wanted slavery to be extended to the new western territories that were attracting settlers and applying for statehood.

Opinions were more divided in the Upper South. Proslavery sentiment was strong in West and Middle Tennessee, where there were many slaves working in cotton fields. East Tennessee, however, had far fewer slaves, and an antislavery movement developed.

In November 1860, Abraham Lincoln was elected US president. Like many Northerners, Lincoln opposed slavery, but he believed it would wither away if it could be kept out of the new territories. Southern slave owners feared Lincoln's election would lead to the end of slavery in their states.

In December 1860, South Carolina seceded—or split—from the United States. Six other states in the Deep South followed, forming the Confederate States of America, or the Confederacy. Several other slave states, including Tennessee, did not immediately join the Confederacy.

In April 1861, Confederate forces bombarded Fort Sumter in Charleston, South Carolina, and President Lincoln called for troops to defend the Union. The Civil War (1861–1865) had begun. By late May three states in the Upper South— Virginia, North Carolina, and Arkansas—had seceded and joined the Confederate side. On June 8, 1861, Tennessee became the last Southern state to join.

Sons on Both Sides

Greenville, Tennessee, is home to the only memorial in that state to honor both Confederate and Union soldiers who died during the Civil War. Greenville was also the home of President Andrew Johnson.

During the Civil War, loyalties in Tennessee were divided. More than 135,000 Tennessee volunteers fought for the South. Nearly 70,000 Tennesseans— including 20,000 African Americans—served with the Union army. Most of Tennessee's Union soldiers were from East Tennessee. There were an estimated 1,400 battles and skirmishes fought in Tennessee, the most in any Southern state except Virginia.

The bloody Battle of Shiloh, fought on April 6–7, 1862, started near the Tennessee River. More than twenty thousand men from the two sides died.

★10★KEY CITIES★ ★ ★

Memphis

Knoxville

1. Memphis: population 646,889

Located on the Mississippi River, Memphis was named after Egypt's former capital, which was along the Nile River. Memphis is known as a cultural center of the South, having given the world such musicians as Elvis Presley, Johnny Cash, and Aretha Franklin.

2. Nashville: population 601,222

The capital of Tennessee, Nashville is located on the banks of the Cumberland River. It is a city of many industries and institutes of higher learning. Nicknamed Music City, Nashville is considered the center of the country music industry.

3. Knoxville: population 178,874

Tennessee's former capital, Knoxville, is the home of the main campus of the University of Tennessee and its popular sports teams, the Volunteers. The Tennessee Valley Authority headquarters is located in Knoxville.

4. Chattanooga: population 167,674

Chattanooga is located in southeastern Tennessee by the Georgia border. It is situated between the Appalachian Mountains and the Cumberland Plateau, giving it such a beautiful mountainous location it is often referred to as the Scenic City.

5. Clarksville: population 132,957

Clarksville, in northern Tennessee, was named after Revolutionary War hero General George Rogers Clark (brother of William Clark of Lewis and Clark). It is the home of the *Leaf-Chronicle*, the oldest newspaper in Tennessee.

TENNESSEE

★ ★ ★ ★ ★

6. Murfreesboro: population 108,755

Murfreesboro is the fastest growing city in Tennessee, and one of the fastest growing cities in the country. It is home of the largest undergraduate university in the state, Middle Tennessee State University.

7. Jackson: population 65,211

Jackson is the seat of Madison County in Western Tennessee. It was originally named Alexandria, but was renamed in 1822 in honor of Andrew Jackson, then a War of 1812 hero, and later President of the United States.

8. Johnson City: population 63,152

Johnson City spreads through three counties: Sullivan, Carter, and Washington. The majority is in Washington County. It has been voted one of the best small cities for businesses and careers, as well as one of the least expensive places to live.

9. Franklin: population 62,487

Franklin is considered part of the Nashville metropolitan area. It was named after inventor and statesman Benjamin Franklin, who was a friend of the city's founder. It has many historical sites, including a Civil War monument.

10. Bartlett: population 54,613

Bartlett is part of the Memphis metropolitan area, sitting northeast of the city. Historically, it was a stop on a major stagecoach route, and later a train depot. Today, it is the site of several historic homes and plantations that attract visitors.

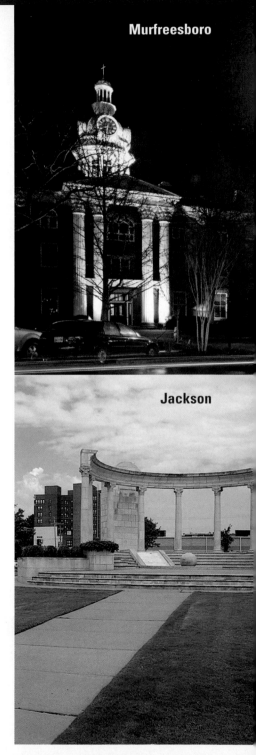

Murfreesboro

Jackson

Tennessean Andrew Johnson stayed loyal to the Union.

Confederate general Albert Sidney Johnston was charged with defending Tennessee from Union forces led by General Ulysses S. Grant. Grant's strategy was to control Tennessee's rivers and railroads in order to prevent supplies from reaching Confederate troops. In February 1862, Grant captured Fort Donelson on the Cumberland River and Fort Henry on the Tennessee River. With Tennessee towns falling into Union hands, Lincoln wanted to make sure citizens obeyed Union laws. In March 1862, he appointed a native Southerner, Andrew Johnson, as military governor. Johnson was a former Tennessee governor who had remained loyal to the Union.

A month later, Union forces won the Battle of Shiloh, at Pittsburg Landing near the Tennessee River. But the battle was bloody for both the North and the South. General Johnston was killed, and historians estimate that more than ten thousand soldiers on each side were killed or wounded.

A key event in favor of the North came in June 1862, when Union forces captured Memphis. With that victory, the North had control of one of the South's leading cotton markets, as well as an important port on the Mississippi. But other battles, big and small, were fought on Tennessee soil over the next two years.

The Civil War came to an end after Confederate general Robert E. Lee surrendered to Grant in Virginia on April 9, 1865. Five days later, President Lincoln was fatally shot while attending a play in Washington, DC. Andrew Johnson, who had been elected vice president in 1864, became the new president.

Reconstruction and Recovery

When Andrew Johnson took office as president, he had the difficult job of trying to rebuild Southern states that had been torn apart by war. Many members of Congress wanted to punish the former Confederate states as conquered enemies. They supported basic rights for the newly freed slaves. These members of Congress also opposed allowing wealthy former slave owners to continue to hold most of the power in Southern states.

However, since Congress was not in session for most of 1865, Johnson put his own **Reconstruction** plan in place. Tennessee and other Southern states had to ratify the Thirteenth Amendment abolishing slavery but had to do little else to rejoin the Union. Johnson's plan also enabled former Confederate leaders to hold positions of power and allowed Southern states to pass laws called the black codes that restricted the rights of African Americans.

Tennessee, like nearly all other Southern states, did what was required and, in December 1865, asked to rejoin the Union. But Congress, now in session, was not ready to seat members from these Southern states. Members of Congress continued to clash with the president over his Reconstruction plan, which they felt forgave the former Confederate states too easily and ignored the plight of former slaves. For example, Johnson rejected (vetoed) a measure requiring states to recognize African Americans as citizens with basic rights. Congress passed that law over his veto, however. It approved an amendment to the US Constitution (the Fourteenth Amendment) that included these rights—and required states to ratify it to rejoin the Union.

African-American Union soldiers flee the Fort Pillow Massacre. Many black soldiers were slaughtered while trying to surrender. The Confederates were led by Nathan Bedford Forrest, a founder of the Ku Klux Klan.

Although many people in Tennessee and other Southern states opposed granting rights to African Americans, those who had sympathized with the Union dominated Tennessee's government in the late 1860s. Unlike other Southern states, Tennessee soon ratified the Fourteenth Amendment, and on July 24, 1866, it became the first Southern state to rejoin the Union.

During the late 1860s, Tennessee's own government took steps to limit the power of former Confederate leaders and to help freed slaves. It extended

Sergeant Alvin York of Pall Mall, Tennessee, received the Congressional Medal of Honor for his heroics in World War I.

voting rights to African-American men. Many citizens strongly resented this action. In 1866, a group of Confederate veterans in Pulaski, Tennessee, formed a secret society called the Ku Klux Klan, which grew quickly and spread to other states. Members, dressed in white hoods and robes, rode out on their horses at night to terrorize African-American community leaders and others. Klan members attacked, whipped, and sometimes killed black people and their supporters. In 1869, Tennessee passed a law calling for the arrest and punishment of any Klan members who engaged in violence. The Ku Klux Klan faded away during the 1870s, though it would return in a new form in the 1920s.

Economically, African Americans were not much better off as free citizens than they were as slaves. Many continued working on the farms of their former slaveholders, putting in long hours for very low pay. Their landlords kept raising rents, causing families to sink into debt.

From the late 1870s and into the 1880s, the newly gained rights of Tennessee's African Americans began to wane. The state legislature passed a law requiring people to pay a fee, or so-called poll tax, to be allowed to vote. It was a great hardship for many of the state's black people, who in effect could not vote because they couldn't afford to pay the tax.

Around the same time, a code of both written and unwritten laws made their way into Tennessee and the other Southern states. Under these so-called Jim Crow laws, black people were segregated, or kept apart, from white people in public places. They had to use separate, often inferior, facilities. African Americans were required to ride in their own railroad cars, eat in their own restaurants, and use their own restrooms and water fountains. African-American students were also barred from attending public schools for white students.

This did not keep Mary Church Terrell from getting an education. The daughter of former slaves was born in Memphis in 1863. She was one of the first African-American women to earn a college degree. Throughout her life Terrell was an activist for civil rights and women's suffrage.

Tennessee was in good economic shape by the end of the nineteenth century. Production of cotton and tobacco, the major crops, soon increased greatly. Iron, coal, and copper mining were also important. Manufacturing was growing, especially in East Tennessee and in the Memphis and Nashville areas. Woolen mills produced textiles, sawmills processed logs, and factories made paper, flour, soap, and other products.

Dumpsters and Tow Trucks

Many everyday things you see on the road were created or first used in Tennessee. The first dumpsters were used in Knoxville in 1935, and soon spread to the rest of the state and eventually the country. Tow trucks were invented in Chattanooga in 1913.

The Early Twentieth Century

By the twentieth century, Tennessee had made great progress. Towns and cities were building schools. Factories were springing up. New roads made it easier for people to market goods and get to work and school.

Textile workers in Elizabethton went on strike for higher wages and equal pay for women in 1929.

In September 1956, twelve black teenagers in Clinton became the first students to integrate a formerly all-white school in the South.

Vietnam War Casualty

Tennessee resident James Davis was long considered to be the first American killed in the Vietnam War. On December 22, 1961 he was killed in an ambush near an air base. There is a monument to him in Livingston. Though it was later discovered that a few other Americans were killed before Davis, he is still honored by his hometown.

In 1917, the United States entered World War I, and more than one hundred thousand Tennesseans joined the armed forces. In support of the war effort, the state's factories became even busier, especially those producing cotton goods, clothing, aluminum, and ammunition.

Starting in 1929, Tennessee and the rest of the nation were hit hard by the **Great Depression**, a time of severe economic hardship. Prices for manufactured goods and produce from the state's farms hit rock bottom. As a result, thousands of people lost their jobs, farms, and homes.

Franklin D. Roosevelt became the thirty-second US president in 1933. He started a series of government programs known as the New Deal to help restore the economy and create jobs. The federally owned Tennessee Valley Authority (TVA) was also created that year to manage the Tennessee River resources to produce cheap electricity, irrigate crops, improve river navigation, and control flooding. The TVA accomplished these goals by constructing thirty-nine **hydroelectric** dams along the river.

Exploding Oak Ridge

Most cities grow fairly slowly. But when the government decided to build a nuclear research facility in Oak Ridge, the area went from sparsely populated woods in 1941 to a city of seventy thousand residents within four years. It was Tennessee's fifth-largest city at the time.

In 1941, after Japanese forces attacked the US Navy base at Pearl Harbor in Hawaii, the nation entered World War II (1939–1945). Some 300,000 Tennesseans served in the armed forces, and close to six thousand lost their lives. Another 280,000 citizens worked in the state's war plants, turning out uniforms, aircraft parts, and other products for the military.

In 1942, the US government bought land in a quiet valley in East Tennessee and ordered local residents to move out. The new town of Oak Ridge, built to house workers and facilities, was surrounded by tight security. It was one of several places around the country where scientists, engineers, and other specialized workers helped produce the world's first atom bomb, as part of the Manhattan Project.

Uranium material produced at the Oak Ridge facilities fueled the first atomic bomb used in war. It was dropped on the Japanese city of Hiroshima on August 6, 1945 and killed more than seventy thousand people. After the war, the Oak Ridge National Laboratory continued as an important research facility, developing peaceful uses for radioactive materials.

Conflict and Change

The 1950s marked a decade of great economic and social change for Tennessee. Many farmers left their fields for opportunities in the larger towns and cities. Tennessee became an industrial state, and the economy grew.

During this time, African Americans began to make gains in their fight against the Jim Crow laws. In 1954, the US Supreme Court—the highest court in the nation—handed down the Brown v. Board of Education decision, which ruled that racially separate schools were inherently unequal and violated the US Constitution. The court ordered that black children be integrated, or admitted, into white schools. In Tennessee, as in other Southern states, there were confrontations between whites and blacks, some of which were violent.

In 1960, Nashville became a center in the movement to end discrimination against African Americans in public facilities. Black college students and others joined in peaceful "sit-ins" at lunch counters where African Americans were not being served. At one point, white people confronted them and fighting broke out. The protesters were arrested and went to jail, but their civil rights movement continued to spread.

Under leaders such as Martin Luther King Jr., a minister from Georgia, African Americans moved toward equal treatment, not only in education but also in public facilities and the workplace. Sadly, Dr. King was assassinated on April 4, 1968, while in Memphis to give support to striking black sanitation workers. His influence, however, lived on in the battle for equal rights.

Mountain Dew

Tennessee is the birthplace of the soft drink Mountain Dew. Invented in 1940 by Tennessee brothers Barney and Ally Hartman, it continues to be popular today. Mountain dew is slang for homemade whiskey, but though this Mountain Dew packs a caffeine punch, it is a non-alcoholic soda.

The Twenty-First Century

As Tennessee entered the twenty-first century, the state had grown economically, socially, and culturally. Today's manufacturing firms in Tennessee provide a variety of jobs. Out-of-staters moving into Tennessee also contribute to a wider mix of traditions, talents, and ideas. The state's outstanding colleges and universities attract students from across the country. In addition, more and more people are exploring Tennessee's picturesque parks, historical sites, and music scene.

Tennessee was hard hit by a nationwide recession, or decline in the economy, which began in late 2007. Though the economy began to recover in 2009, progress has been uneven. In September 2014, Tennessee had a 6.6 percent unemployment rate, slightly higher than the national average of 5.7 percent at that time. But Tennessee continues to attract new companies to the state, particularly in automobile manufacturing, and the job market has shown improvement.

10 KEY DATES IN STATE HISTORY

1. 12,000 BCE

The first humans settle in present-day Tennessee. Early hunter-gatherers are replaced by the Mound Builders, and later by tribes such as the Cherokee and Chickasaw.

2. April 9, 1682

René-Robert Cavelier, sieur de La Salle, claims the Mississippi Valley for France.

3. February 10, 1763

The French and Indian War ends with the signing of the Treaty of Paris. Great Britain gains almost all of France's land east of the Mississippi River, including what is now Tennessee.

4. June 1, 1796

Tennessee becomes the sixteenth US state, with Knoxville established as its first capital.

5. May 28, 1830

The signing of the Indian Removal Act forces members of the Cherokee tribes to give up their lands in Tennessee.

6. June 8, 1861

After the Civil War begins, Tennessee becomes the last Southern state to join the Confederacy. When the war is over in 1866, Tennessee is the first Southern state to rejoin the Union.

7. May 18, 1933

US president Franklin D. Roosevelt establishes the Tennessee Valley Authority (TVA).

8. April 4, 1968

Civil rights leader Martin Luther King Jr. is shot on the balcony of his hotel room in Memphis. The killing sets off riots across the country. The man convicted of his murder, James Earl Ray, dies in a Tennessee prison on April 23, 1998.

9. November 3, 1992

Tennessee politician Al Gore is elected vice president of the United States under Bill Clinton. He served two terms.

10. April 25–28, 2011

Massive tornado outbreak hits the South, killing thirty-two in Tennessee.

Stars and street performers help Nashville live up to its nickname, Music City.

The People

3

More than six million people live in Tennessee today. It ranks seventeenth in population among the fifty states. About 95 percent of Tennessee's residents were born in the United States. The majority of residents are native to the state, with about three out of every five residents having been born in Tennessee. Many of today's Tennesseans are descendants of the state's early settlers.

After the end of the French and Indian War in 1763, colonists from the Carolinas, Virginia, and Pennsylvania became very interested in the fertile land between the Appalachian Mountains and the Mississippi River, which had become British territory as a result of the war. Within a few years, hardy pioneers began settling in the Watauga River valley and then in other parts of the region. Most of these colonists were of English heritage. Many others were Scots-Irish, which means they traced their origins to Scottish and English Protestant families that had gone to the northern part of Ireland in the 1600s. Others were of Irish or German heritage. The early settlers and their descendants farmed, worked in the towns, and started businesses big and small.

According to the 2010 Census, Caucasians—or white people—now make up about 78 percent of the state's population. Many of today's Tennesseans do not describe themselves as any particular nationality as far as their ancestry, considering themselves simply

American when they are polled. However, about 15 percent call themselves English, Scots, Scots-Irish, or Welsh. Another 11 percent describe themselves as Irish, while 10 percent say they are of German ancestry. Other Tennesseans trace their origins to Italy, France, the Netherlands, Scandinavia, and other parts of Europe.

The foreign-born population in the state has nearly doubled in the past twenty years. Almost half of all foreign-born Tennesseans come from Latin America, and most of the rest come from Asia. These people have helped make the state grow and prosper while contributing their own cultures and traditions.

African Americans

African Americans make up by far the largest minority group in Tennessee. When white settlers came to the region—particularly in the western section of what is now Tennessee—hundreds of years ago, they brought black slaves with them, mostly to work in the fields. By 1840, more than 180,000 black slaves lived in Tennessee, about a quarter of the state's entire population. Approximately five thousand free blacks lived in the state. After the Civil War ended, Tennessee's black population continued to increase, as freed slaves from Virginia, North Carolina, and South Carolina came to the state.

During the first half of the twentieth century, many African Americans in Tennessee and other Southern states moved from rural areas to cities, often to the cities of the North,

Musicians bring the blues to Beale Street in Memphis.

for better job opportunities. African Americans today make up about 17 percent of Tennessee's total population, compared to about 24 percent in 1900. The largest African-American populations in the state today are in and around Memphis.

Throughout the state's history, African Americans have helped to build, populate, and enhance Tennessee communities. To give just one example, African-American workers were responsible for constructing nearly every major building that went up in East Tennessee's Sevier County during the late nineteenth and early twentieth centuries. Tennessee's African Americans have also made important contributions to culture. The roots of the blues and rock 'n' roll can be traced directly to the African-American community in Memphis.

Other Minorities

Hispanics, who may be of any race, make up close to 5 percent of the state's population. Tennessee now has almost three hundred thousand people of Hispanic, or Latino, heritage. The majority of them trace their roots to Mexico. Large numbers are of Puerto Rican or Cuban heritage. Hispanic Americans are Tennessee's fastest-growing cultural group. Between 2000 and 2010, the state's Hispanic population more than doubled. Many Hispanics moved into the Nashville area and other big cities, attracted by job opportunities.

Tennessee's population of Asian Americans and people from the Pacific islands is much smaller, but these groups also grew in size significantly—by more than 60 percent—between 2000 and 2010. Among the new Asian immigrants are many people from India.

Some newer immigrants have either feared or suffered persecution in other countries. Nashville has a Kurdish community called Little Kurdistan. Many of its residents are refugees who fled from Iraq to escape persecution when Iraqi leader Saddam Hussein was in power. As conflicts in the region continue, other refugees continue to make their way to the area. A number of refugees from Somalia have resettled in parts of Middle Tennessee, including Shelbyville, where many work in the chicken processing plant.

Lincoln Museum

The Abraham Lincoln Library and Museum is located in Harrogate, a former Confederate town. The museum features one of the largest and strangest Abe Lincoln collections. It has odd artistic representations of Honest Abe as an Easter Island head, a clown, and Superman. It also has scholarly and historic Lincoln **memorabilia**.

★ 10 KEY PEOPLE ★ ★ ★

1. Miley Cyrus

Born Destiny Hope Cyrus in Franklin in 1992, the daughter of singer Billy Ray Cyrus gained fame on the popular television show *Hannah Montana*. That led to a singing career. In July 2014, Miley ranked number seventeen on a list of the most powerful celebrities.

Miley Cyrus

2. Nikki Giovanni

Born in Knoxville in 1943, Nikki Giovanni graduated from Fisk University in 1968 after publishing the first of many books of poetry, *Black Feeling, Black Talk*. Her popular poems often express black pride and love of family.

3. Jack Hanna

Zookeeper and television personality Jack Hanna was born in Knoxville in 1947. He often gives live animal demonstrations on TV shows such as *Late Night with David Letterman* and *Good Morning America*. He is known for his safari clothes and Southern accent.

Jack Hanna

4. Benjamin Hooks

Benjamin Hooks was a minister and civil rights attorney born in Memphis. He was the executive director of the National Association for the Advancement of Colored People (NAACP) from 1977 to 1992. He received the Presidential Medal of Freedom in 2007.

5. Casey Jones

Jonathan Luther Jones, known as Casey, was a train engineer who died in 1900 when his train, the Cannonball Express, crashed. His heroic efforts to save passengers were immortalized in the folk song, "The Ballad of Casey Jones."

Benjamin Hooks

TENNESSEE

6. Dolly Parton

Tennessee native Dolly Parton was born into poverty, but she rose to become one of the biggest country music stars and owner of Dollywood, the theme park in Pigeon Forge. She is also a philanthropist, supporting children's literacy in particular.

7. Elvis Presley

The King of Rock 'n' Roll was born in Mississippi in 1935, but he moved to Memphis as a teenager. That's where his music career began. In addition to recording numerous hits, such as "Jailhouse Rock," "Hound Dog," and "Blue Suede Shoes," he acted and sang in movies.

8. Wilma Rudolph

Wilma Rudolph contracted polio and had to wear a brace on her leg as a child, yet earned the nickname "the world's fastest woman." She became the first American woman to win three gold medals at one Olympics, at the age of twenty in Rome in 1960.

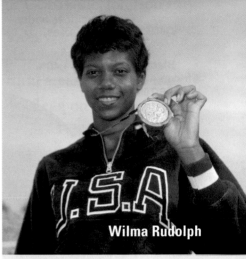
Wilma Rudolph

9. Sequoyah

Born around 1770 in eastern Tennessee, Sequoyah developed eighty-five symbols for the syllables in spoken Cherokee, enabling the language to be written for the first time. Soon the Cherokee had a higher literacy rate than the settlers on the frontier.

Sequoyah

10. Taylor Swift

Taylor Swift was born in Pennsylvania in 1989 but moved with her family to Tennessee at the age of fourteen. The Country Music Association named her Entertainer of the Year in 2009, and she has won seven Grammy Awards.

Taylor Swift

The congregation of the Suggs Creek Cumberland Presbyterian Church was organized circa 1800.

Religion

Many religions are represented in Tennessee today, and many other residents don't follow any religion at all. The majority of the population—82 percent—consider themselves Christians. Of those, 70 percent are Protestants. Among the Protestants, 39 percent are Baptists. The Southern Baptist Convention has the largest number of followers, numbering 1,483,356 in 2010. Other Protestant denominations in Tennessee are Methodists at 10 percent, Presbyterian at 3 percent, Church of God at 2 percent, Lutheran at 2 percent, and Pentecostal at 2 percent.

Other Christian religious practices in Tennessee include the Church of Christ, with 6 percent of the population practicing, and Roman Catholic, with 6 percent of the population practicing. A further 12 percent identify themselves as Christians without specifying any other affiliation.

One percent of the population follows Islam. Two percent of the population follows other religions. Nine percent of the Tennessee population does not follow any religion. These may be atheists or agnostics.

Income and Housing

The average per capita income—or the income for each individual—between 2008 and 2012 was $24,294. The median household income for Tennessee residents during that same time period was $44,140. (In Tennessee there are an average of 2.51 people in every household.) In the 2008 to 2012 time period, 17.3 people were below the mean poverty level. The amount below which a person can be considered to live in poverty varies, but as an example, in 2014 a family of four would be considered below the poverty level if the household income was less than $23,850 per year. Tennessee's total is about 2 percentage points above the national average.

Many Tennessee residents are homeowners. In 2013 there were 2,843,914 total housing units in Tennessee. About 18.2 of those are in multi-unit structures, including condominiums. In the period between 2008 and 2012, 68.4 percent of families lived in homes that they owned. (Some of those were completely paid for, while others had been secured with a mortgage, or a loan from the bank, and were in the process of being paid off.) The median home value in the 2008 to 2012 period was $138,700.

Business Ownership

In 2007 there were 545,348 business firms in Tennessee, owned and operated by a diverse assortment of people. In 2007, women owned 25.7 percent of those firms. African Americans owned 8.4 percent of the firms, which is higher than the national average of 7.1 percent. Hispanic residents own 1.6 percent of the firms in Tennessee, far lower than the national average of 8.3 percent. Asian-owned firms account for 2 percent, while about 0.5 percent of firms are owned by Native Americans or by Alaskan Natives. People of Native Hawaiian and other Pacific Islander backgrounds own the smallest number of firms, at just 0.1 percent.

Tennesseans Today

Tennesseans are known for being passionate about many things. One of them is the love of the outdoors. The Tennessee woods offer hunters many kinds of game. The state's lakes and streams provide plenty of good fishing, and Tennesseans enjoy hiking and camping in state parks and national parks and forests. Tennessee residents on the whole love getting outside and into nature.

Sports are also popular with the people of Tennessee. Fans root for professional teams, including the Nashville-based Tennessee Titans in the National Football League (NFL), the Memphis Grizzlies in the National Basketball Association (NBA), and the Nashville Predators in the National Hockey League (NHL). The Bristol Motor Speedway is one of the biggest sports venues in the nation. Popular college sports teams include the University of Tennessee Volunteers and Lady Vols, University of Memphis Tigers, and Vanderbilt Commodores. College football's Liberty Bowl is played every year in Memphis.

10 KEY EVENTS

Bonnaroo

Dogwood Arts Festival

1. Africa in April

During the third week of April, Memphis hosts a festival celebrating the arts, crafts, culture, and history of the African diaspora (or the scattering of people from their homeland). Each year, a different nation is celebrated.

2. Bonnaroo

Bonnaroo is a four-day music festival held on a 700-acre (283 ha) farm in Manchester. Though it started out with jam bands and folk rock, it now features many kinds of music, such as country, pop, reggae, hip-hop, and indie rock.

3. Dogwood Arts Festival

This festival in Knoxville in April offers displays of sidewalk art and tours of homes, gardens, and trails. Visitors also get the chance to enjoy the city's beautiful dogwoods, azaleas, and other flowering plants—and eat fried treats called funnel cakes.

4. Fall Festival and State Pow Wow

Each October in Nashville, Native Americans gather to share aspects of their culture. Visitors can sample Native American foods, buy or admire jewelry, paintings, pottery, and clothing, and enjoy storytelling and games.

5. Great Tennessee Air Show

This event, held in mid-June in Smyrna, was recognized as one of the "Top 10 Best Air Shows in the World" by *USA Today*. It features acrobatic flying, military and civilian aircraft, and a Kid Zone.

TENNESSEE ★ ★ ★ ★

Rhododendron Festival

6. Mule Day

Columbia has been celebrating all things mule-related since 1840. Now, this four-day, springtime festival features mule-driving contests and awards for the best mules, as well as music, crafts, food, lumberjack events, storytelling competitions, and the Liar's Contest.

7. Rhododendron Festival

This festival, held at the foot of Roan Mountain on the third weekend in June, pays tribute to one of Tennessee's most colorful flowering plants. The two-day event also features crafts, traditional mountain music, and old-time folkway demonstrations.

8. Riverbend Festival

This nine-day event, held in Chattanooga in June, features live music by rock, country, bluegrass, and other bands, as well as food, fireworks, and attractions including a children's village.

Riverbend Festival

9. Tennessee State Fair

Since 1869, people from all over the state have been meeting, eating, and competing at this September event in Nashville. The fair offers all kinds of craft and agricultural displays, carnival rides, and live entertainment, not to mention corn dogs and plenty of other food.

10. West Tennessee Strawberry Festival

A celebration of small-town America, the West Tennessee Strawberry Festival is a weeklong event held in Humboldt in early May. It includes parades, a carnival, street dancing, beauty pageants, and West Tennessee strawberries.

The Tennessee State Capitol was completed in 1859.

How the Government Works

4

Tennessee has about 350 cities and towns. Each city or town has its own government—often headed by a mayor and a council—responsible for police and fire protection, schools, libraries, sanitation, and other basic services. The state is also divided into ninety-five counties. County governments are responsible for managing elections, collecting taxes, registering property titles, enforcing education laws, maintaining courts, and other local duties. Most of Tennessee's counties are governed by a county executive and a board of county commissioners.

Three of Tennessee's counties have a combined city-county form of government. The largest is Nashville–Davidson County, formed by a merger in 1963. Besides Nashville, Davidson County includes seven smaller cities or towns. The combined government, run by a mayor and a council, is responsible for most city and county duties, but the seven smaller municipalities are in charge of some duties on their own, including police protection.

The state government is responsible for matters that affect Tennessee as a whole. Education, transportation, the environment, business and economic growth, and public health and safety are some areas where the state has a major role to play. Like the federal government and other state governments, Tennessee's state government is divided into three branches: executive, legislative, and judicial. Each branch has its own responsibilities. The governor heads the executive branch. The state's senators and representatives make up the legislative, or law-making, branch. The judicial branch is made up of judges who are in charge of the different state courts. Most of the people involved in state government work in Nashville, the state capital.

The state also has representatives at the national level. Tennessee voters elect two US senators to serve six-year terms in Washington, DC. Tennesseans also elect nine members of the House of Representatives to serve two-year terms. These federal legislators represent Tennessee's interests and concerns regarding national issues.

Branches of Government

Executive

The head of the executive branch is the governor. He or she is elected to a four-year term by state voters and may not serve more than two terms in a row. The governor runs the state government, puts together the state budget, and approves or vetoes (rejects) measures that were passed by lawmakers. The governor also appoints the heads of twenty-one cabinet-level departments, which carry out state government functions.

In Their Own Words

"Be always sure you are right—then go ahead."
—Davy Crockett

Legislative

Tennessee's legislative branch consists of a general assembly made up of two chambers, or houses: a thirty-three-member Senate and ninety-nine-member House of Representatives. Senators serve four-year terms, while members of the House of Representatives serve two-year terms. There are no limits on the number of terms legislators may serve. Tennessee's general assembly passes new state laws or changes existing laws. Members also elect Tennessee's secretary of state, treasurer, and comptroller. The state senate elects a speaker, who also has the title of lieutenant governor and becomes governor if the current governor dies or resigns.

Judicial

The state's highest court is the Tennessee Supreme Court. It hears appeals of important cases decided by lower courts and also interprets the laws and constitution of Tennessee. The supreme court can overturn a law if it concludes that the law violates the state constitution. The court is made up of five justices who serve eight-year terms and are elected by the people. The justices themselves select one of their members to serve as chief justice, and they elect an attorney general, who serves an eight-year term.

The state also has a court of appeals that hears appeals from trial courts and certain state boards and commissions in civil cases (involving disputes between people or companies), and a separate court of appeals for criminal cases. Each of these courts has twelve members who sit in panels of three and meet monthly.

Silly Law

In Tennessee, it is illegal to lasso a fish. You can only catch fish there with a rod and reel, so other methods—like using your teeth, a harpoon, or dynamite—are also against the law.

There are various kinds of trial courts at the county level and for each of the state's thirty-one judicial districts. Specialized trial courts deal with juvenile issues and family matters. In addition, municipal courts in the towns and cities handle matters such as traffic offenses and violations of local laws.

How a Bill Becomes a Law

Tennessee has a specific procedure for making laws. Ideas for laws can come from any resident of the state, but it is up to the state's senators or representatives to introduce any proposed law, or bill, in the legislature. That is what starts a bill on the way to possibly becoming law.

The general assembly meets in the capitol to discuss legislation.

The senator or representative proposing a bill gives it to the chief clerk. He or she examines the measure to make sure it follows legislative rules. Then, the bill is given a number. According to Tennessee law, every bill needs to be considered on three different days in each chamber, or house, of the general assembly.

The bill first goes back to the chamber where it was proposed. If there is no objection to the bill after this first reading, it gets a second reading the next day. After that, it is sent to a standing committee, a group of legislators who have experience in a certain area. For example, a bill about the state's agriculture will be given to a committee of legislators who are familiar with agricultural issues and laws.

If the standing committee approves the bill, it goes to a scheduling committee. In the senate, this committee merely decides when the measure should go back to the full senate. In the house, this committee can also decide whether to pass it along or not.

March of the Ducks

The Peabody Hotel in Memphis has been home to mallard ducks since 1933. Since 1940, the hotel has hosted the "March of the Ducks" twice each day. A Duckmaster leads the ducks from their rooftop home, down a special elevator, through the lobby to their own personal fountain. At night the Duckmaster leads them home again.

Once the measure gets back to the house or senate for the third time, it is open for debate and amendments (changes). In order to be passed, with or without changes, it must be approved by a majority of all members—that is, by fifty or more votes in the house or by seventeen or more in the senate. If the legislators in one chamber pass the bill on the third reading, it is sent to the other chamber. There, the same process takes place.

If the second chamber passes the bill without changes, then the bill is ready to go to the governor. But if the second chamber amends the bill before passing it, then the amended version goes back to the first house. If the first house does not accept the amendments, then the bill goes to a conference committee. This committee, made up of members from each house, tries to come up with a compromise version that both houses will accept.

When a bill passes both houses in exactly the same form, it is sent to the governor, who has ten days to either sign or veto it. If he or she signs the bill, it becomes law. If the measure is vetoed, it can still become law, provided that a majority of the membership of

Tennesseans made their voices heard in 2011 when they protested against plans to build a nuclear weapons plant in Oak Ridge.

both houses votes to override the veto. If the governor takes no action within ten days of receiving a bill, it automatically becomes law.

Making Your Voice Heard

Once you reach the age of eighteen, you will be able to vote in state and federal elections. In the meantime, you can do your best to learn about the history of your state and nation, recent events of importance, and the issues that elected officials must decide. The more informed you are, the better you can fulfill your responsibilities as a citizen and voter.

You can also make your voice heard. If you know about an issue in your community or state, you can discuss it with people who are able to vote and also contact your legislators to share your views. These government officials are there to help and represent you, and to make your state a better place to live. They expect to hear from the people they serve and are interested in gaining the loyalty and trust of people who may—or may not—vote for them in the future.

POLITICAL ★ FIGURES
FROM TENNESSEE

★ Davy Crockett:
US Congress, 1827-1831, 1833-1835

Born in 1786 in Greene County, this "King of the Wild Frontier" was a skilled hunter and woodsman, as well as a storyteller. Although he had fought in battles against Native Americans, he spoke out strongly against President Andrew Jackson's Indian Removal Act. He was killed in 1836 in the Battle of the Alamo, in the war for Texas's Independence from Mexico.

★ Al Gore Jr.: US Vice President, 1993-2001

Al Gore Jr.'s family was from Tennessee, but he was born in 1948 in Washington, DC, while his father was serving in congress. He served in both the House of Representatives and the Senate from 1977 to 1993, then served two terms as vice president. In 2000, he lost a close presidential election. Gore became an environmental activist, winning a Nobel Peace Prize in 2007.

★ A C Wharton Jr.: Memphis Mayor, 2009-

Born in Lebanon, Tennessee, Wharton earned degrees in politics and law and spent twenty-five years teaching before entering politics. He became mayor of Shelby County, then was elected mayor of Memphis in a special election in 2009. His focus has been on crime prevention, job creation, and economic growth.

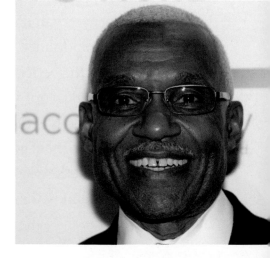

TENNESSEE
YOU CAN MAKE A DIFFERENCE

Contacting Lawmakers

Even before you are old enough to vote, you can take an active interest in politics and the laws that affect you and your community. You can make your voice heard by contacting Tennessee lawmakers.

To find contact information for Tennessee legislators, go to **www.capitol.tn.gov/legislators**

There, you can find information about current legislation. In addition, under "Find Legislators," if you type in your address and click "submit," you will be told who your state legislators are.In most cases, all you need to do is type your street address into the boxes under Find My Legislator. This will take you to a web page that should show the correct name and contact information for your state senator and state representative.

You can find contact information for your US representatives by visiting **www.opencongress.org/people/zipcodelookup** and typing in your ZIP code.

Protecting People Who Save Kids

Every year, an estimated thirty-eight children in the United States die from being locked in a hot car. The dark portions of the car that absorb heat, such as a dark dashboard or seat, can reach 200 degrees Fahrenheit (93.3 degrees Celsius). A human will suffer from heatstroke when his or her body temperature reaches 104°F (40°C). When the core body temperature reaches 107°F (41.6°C), cells are damaged, organs shut down, and a person can die. Children overheat faster than adults.

Tennesseans can rescue children from hot cars without fear of being sued.

Tennessee activists wanted a law to encourage people to check parked cars and to take action to save a child. Some activists were concerned that passers-by would be afraid of being **sued** for damaging a car if they broke a window to save a child.

Working with organizations like Kids And Cars, Tennessee activists encouraged Tennessee State Representative David Hawk to sponsor a bill that would keep good Samaritans free from liability. Now it has become a law. Anyone acting to save a child won't be sued for damages.

Thousands of people build automobiles in Tennessee in plants such as this one operated by General Motors.

Making a Living

From the early eighteenth century until well into the twentieth century, Tennessee's economy was based mostly on agriculture. That began to change around the mid-1930s. Dams created by the Tennessee Valley Authority (TVA) helped harness the power of the Tennessee River to produce electricity. This created an inexpensive source of energy for factories. Manufacturing companies began moving to the region. In addition, improvements in roads and in navigating the state's rivers made it easier for manufacturers to ship goods in and out of the state. Tennessee became more of an industrial state. Beginning in the 1980s, as more people began moving into Tennessee from other states, the number of retail outlets, specialty shops, banks, and other service-oriented businesses started to increase significantly.

Agriculture and Mining

A small number of Tennesseans own or work on farms today, but agriculture continues to play an important role in the state's economy. The state now has around eighty thousand farms. Tennessee farmers raise cattle and chickens. Soybeans are a valuable crop and major export. Corn, hay, cotton, tobacco, wheat, and greenhouse plants are also among the biggest sources of farm income.

Tobacco is still an important crop on Tennessee's farms.

Each of the state's three regions—East, Middle, and West Tennessee—grows different crops. The fertile flatland areas of West Tennessee, enriched by silt from the Mississippi River, are perfect for growing cotton and soybeans. The area is also dotted with peach and apple orchards. Middle Tennessee, with its nutrient-rich soil and gently sloping hills, is ideal for raising beef and dairy cattle as well as sheep. Many animals graze on its grassy fields. Among the chief crops that are grown in this region, particularly in the Nashville Basin area, are wheat, potatoes, apples, and pears. East Tennessee is well suited for growing tobacco, snap beans, tomatoes, cabbage, and strawberries.

Tennessee also has a wide variety of valuable minerals. Some of the metals mined in the state are copper, lead, manganese, iron, gold, and zinc. The state is a leader in zinc production, with large deposits in parts of East and Middle Tennessee. Tennessee's major nonmetal mining products include limestone and coal. Limestone is used in buildings, and crushed limestone is used in manufacturing concrete and in paving roads. Limestone deposits are concentrated in the eastern section of the state. Most of the coal comes from the Appalachian Plateau.

Manufacturing

Manufacturing in Tennessee did not begin to grow significantly until after the TVA programs of the 1930s attracted many companies. Industry continued to grow after World War II. Beginning in the 1980s, a number of high-tech companies, including a few Japanese electronics firms, moved into the state to set up production facilities. For that reason, Tennessee is sometimes dubbed the Silicon Valley of the South. ("Silicon Valley" refers to a part of California that is known for its technology industry.)

The Gibson Guitar Corporation has its headquarters in Nashville.

Automakers, especially foreign-owned companies, also began manufacturing cars and trucks in Tennessee and other Southern states. Nissan launched its first US production plant in Smyrna in 1983. In 2011, Volkswagen opened a factory in Chattanooga, and in 2014 announced it would add two thousand more jobs at the plant to build a new SUV. General Motors, in 2009, closed its assembly plant in Spring Hill, which had produced the now-defunct Saturn brand of cars since 1990. But it reopened in 2012, and now employs nearly two thousand people.

Today, manufacturing makes up about 13 percent of Tennessee's gross state product, which is the total value of goods and services created by the state. Besides electronic products and motor vehicles and parts, Tennessee factories also turn out foods and beverages, metal products, chemicals, appliances and electrical equipment, machinery, paper, and plastic and rubber products, among other goods. Manufacturing jobs declined sharply during the recession, or downturn in the economy, that began in late 2007. After 2009, manufacturing jobs, especially in the production of "durable goods"—those meant to last a long time—began to show improvement.

While the growth of manufacturing over the years has created many jobs, factories often use or create chemicals and waste products that can harm the environment and

★ 10 KEY INDUSTRIES ★

Agriculture

Energy Production

1. Agriculture

With more than 44 percent of Tennessee consisting of farmland, agriculture is one of the top industries in the state. Soybeans are by far the biggest crop, followed by corn, cotton, and tobacco. Nursery and greenhouse products are also important.

2. Energy Production

The Tennessee Valley Authority has eleven coal-fired generators and 106 natural gas-fired generators producing energy. It also maintains twenty-nine hydroelectric dams. More recently, Tennessee has started working with alternative energy sources.

3. Food Manufacturing

Processed foods are the largest sector of Tennessee's manufacturing industry. Processed grain products such as bread and breakfast cereals are especially important. Drink manufacturing is also big for both alcohol and soft drinks.

4. Health Care

Nashville is the country's health care central. Twenty-one of the state's 350 health care companies are in the city. Related firms that specialize in meeting the needs of the health care industry, such as legal and accounting firms, also thrive.

5. Livestock

One of the main sources of agricultural income in Tennessee is livestock. Cattle raised for beef are the main component, followed by broiler chickens, pigs, chickens raised for eggs, and dairy cows. Riding horses, such as the famous Tennessee walking horse, are also raised here.

TENNESSEE

Music

Vehicle Manufacturing

6. Mining

Limestone mining provides the largest chunk of Tennessee's mining economy. A lot of the rock is used for building roads, and for cement. Coal is next in economic import, followed by zinc mining and clays, sand, gravel, and phosphate.

7. Music

Music is one of the most valuable products produced in Tennessee. The city of Nashville has become synonymous with country music, and the local music scene has generated billions of dollars for the local and state economy. There are about two hundred recording studios in Nashville.

8. Tourism

From Graceland to Dollywood, from metropolitan Nashville to the eastern mountains, Tennessee offers something for a wide range of tourists. In 2012, tourism generated $16 billion and employed nearly 150,000 Tennesseans.

9. Transportation and Logistics

Transportation and logistics industries involve all facets of moving goods from one place to another. It includes trucking industries, as well as other methods of transport. Seventy-five percent of US markets are located within a one-day drive of Tennessee. FedEx has its home base in Tennessee.

10. Vehicle Manufacturing

Tennessee has a large manufacturing industry, and one of the biggest aspects involves making such vehicles as cars, trucks, and aircraft. Tennessee is home to motor vehicle assembly plants for Volkswagen, Nissan, and General Motors.

Recipe for Tennessee Spoon Bread

The South is known for a unique food called Spoon Bread. Not really a bread, this cornmeal concoction is more like a Yorkshire pudding or a cornbread souffle. You can make a sweet version and top it with maple syrup, but this is a savory version with sharp cheddar cheese.

What You Need

3 cups (710 milliliters) of milk

3 eggs

1½ cups (355 mL) of cornmeal

1 cup (236 mL) of sharp cheddar cheese (shredded or grated)

3 tablespoons (44 mL) of butter

2 teaspoons (10 mL) of baking powder

½ teaspoon (2.5 mL) of salt

A casserole or baking dish

What to Do

- Preheat the oven to 375°F (177°C).
- Get an adult to help you bring the milk to a boil, reduce the heat, and gradually add the cornmeal, stirring constantly. Continue to stir for several minutes until the mixture is smooth.
- Remove the mixture from the heat and let it cool for a few minutes. Beat the eggs, then mix in the butter, cheese, baking powder, and salt. (Butter may be softened to room temperature or melted slightly in the microwave to make mixing easier.) Beat the combined mixture with a hand or electric mixer for several minutes.
- Pour the mix into a well-greased casserole. Bake for 30 to 35 minutes, until the top is golden brown and the mix has set.
- Serve Tennessee Spoon Bread warm as a main dish or a side. It is great for breakfast with bacon and eggs, for lunch with veggies, or for dinner with traditional Tennessee barbecue.

human health. The state of Tennessee has about a dozen sites known to have high amounts of dangerous waste. Residents who live near the sites are worried that chemicals are entering the water and soil, killing plants and animals and endangering human health. Sites that are placed on the national Superfund list—the federal government's program to clean up the nation's uncontrolled hazardous waste sites—are being cleaned up or are scheduled to be cleaned up.

Air pollution is another problem in Tennessee, mainly because of toxic substances released into the air from coal-fired power plants and from chemical plants. However, air quality has been improving, as steps are taken to reduce these emissions. Concerned citizens, business owners, and government officials have worked together in this and other ways so that the state can have a clean environment and continue to develop economically.

Providing Services

Most of Tennessee's workers do not work on farms or in factories. They provide some kind of service, as opposed to growing a crop or making a product. Workers in so-called service industries include salesclerks, barbers, restaurant workers, and real estate agents. About 12 percent of Tennessee's working population has jobs in retail stores.

Vinyl Lives!

Many young people don't remember the days of vinyl, and might never have used a record or record player, but that way of recording music isn't dead yet. Nashville is the home of United Record Pressing, one of only four vinyl record makers left in the country.

Education and health care are the biggest combined sectors in Tennessee's economy, employing about 23 percent of the workforce. Many of these people are teachers, principals, doctors, nurses, or technicians. Another 9 percent of the labor force work as managers or scientists or practice a profession, such as architecture or law.

Some Tennesseans work on stage or in a recording studio. Blues music, which had its earliest beginnings in African-American communities in the Deep South, was widely popular as early as 1909, when W. C. Handy moved his band to Beale Street in Memphis. Country music came to life in the mountains of eastern Tennessee during the late 1920s. A section of Nashville called Music Row has been known worldwide since the 1950s for its record companies, music-publishing houses, recording studios, and music clubs. Over the years, country artists such as Johnny Cash, Carl Perkins, and Dolly Parton performed or recorded songs in Nashville, giving the city its nickname of Music City USA. Their recordings and performances, including radio spots on Nashville's Grand Ole Opry, have made country music one of the most popular music styles in the nation.

Tourism

Another important service industry in Tennessee is tourism. The tourist industry provides jobs for many thousands of Tennesseans. Tennessee businesses—and the state, because of tax revenues—benefit from the billions of dollars tourists spend each year on meals, lodging, activities, souvenirs, and the like.

Throughout the year, people come to hike and camp in Tennessee's wilderness areas or to enjoy boating and swimming. The 521,000-acre (211,000 ha) Great Smoky Mountains National Park in East Tennessee contains some of the most scenic areas in eastern North America. Its streams, meadows, forests, and spectacular waterfalls are a treat for residents and visitors.

The Lost Sea Adventure

Located beneath Sweetwater, Tennessee, the Lost Sea Adventure takes visitors underground into the caverns to see America's largest underwater lake. There is even a glass bottom boat to tour the lake.

The state has many fascinating historical sites. Chickamauga and Chattanooga National Military Park, near Lookout Mountain—the site of the Civil War battle in 1863—is the largest and oldest US military park. Other popular historic sites include a restored Chucalissa Native American village in Memphis, President Andrew Johnson's homestead in Greeneville, and President Andrew Jackson's estate, the Hermitage, near Nashville. Nashville's Tennessee State Museum, founded in 1937, features Davy Crockett's powder horn and Andrew Jackson's top hat.

You can also visit Graceland, the home of Elvis Presley, in Memphis, as well as Beale Street, the entertainment district where blues music blossomed in the early 1900s. Way east, in the Great Smoky Mountains area, is Dollywood, a theme park named after the country singer Dolly Parton. In Nashville, you can visit the home of the Grand Ole Opry and the Country Music Hall of Fame.

Products and Resources

The Volunteer State plays a key role in the manufacture of chemical products. These are used to make things such as soap, paints, synthetic fibers, medicines, and explosive materials.

The Grand Ole Opry has drawn the best country music performers since 1925.

Cotton has long been big in Tennessee. Some 7,000 acres (3,000 ha) were harvested for cotton in 1801. By 1821, that number had jumped to 130,000 acres (50,000 ha), making cotton among the state's chief cash crops. Today, even more land is devoted to cotton, and in most years, well over five hundred thousand bales of cotton are produced.

Tennessee "marble" is a pinkish-gray limestone found in East Tennessee. First quarried in 1838, it is about 460 million years old. It has been used in constructing many monuments and public buildings, including the National Air and Space Museum and parts of the US Capitol in Washington, DC.

Tennessee has had hard economic times and faces challenges ahead. But thanks to the early pioneers and many generations of families and workers, a remote frontier region has been transformed into a bustling state with factories and sprawling farmland, big cities and small towns, many different industries, and millions of residents.

TENNESSEE
STATE MAP

Reelfoot National Wildlife Refuge
Land Between the Lakes
Port Royal State Historic Area
Big South Fork National River and Recreation Area
Chuck Swan Forest and Wildlife Management Area

Kingsport
Bristol
Union City
Paris
Kentucky Lake
Lake Barkley
Cumberland River
Springfield
Portland
Gallatin
La Follette
Norris Lake
Clinch River
Cherokee Lake
Johnson City
Elizabethton
Reelfoot Lake
McKenzie
Nashville
Cookeville
Oak Ridge
Morristown
Greeneville
Appalachian Trail
Big Cypress Tree State Natural Area
Natchez Trace State Park and Forest
Dyersburg
Dickson
Tennessee River
Percy Priest Lake
Catoosa Wildlife Management Area
Crossville
Knoxville
Douglas Lake
Humboldt
Smyrna
Franklin
Murfreesboro
Rockwood
Maryville
Pigeon Forge
Moss Island State Waterfowl Refuge
Ripley
Duck River
Watts Bar Lake
Tellico Lake
Clingmans Dome
Brownsville
Jackson
McMinnville
Dayton
Cherokee National Forest
Great Smoky Mountains National Park
Pinson Mounds State Archaeological Park
Columbia
Lewisburg
Manchester
Appalachian Mountains
Whiteville
Savannah
Old Stone Forest State Archaeological Area
Chickamauga Lake
Memphis
Pulaski
Tims Ford Lake
Lawrenceburg
Tullahoma
Winchester
Chickamauga & Chattanooga National Military Park
Cleveland
Chattanooga
Collierville
Fayetteville
Mississippi River

Legend
- Interstate Highway
- U.S. Highway
- State Highway
- ★ State Capital
- City or Town
- National Forest
- State Park
- Wildlife Refuge
- Recreation Area
- Highest Point in the State
- Mountains
- National Park
- Historic Area

miles
0   30

N
W   E
S

TENNESSEE
MAP SKILLS

1. Which major city is at the intersections of Interstates 40, 24, and 65?

2. The popular tourist destination Pigeon Forge is in which national park?

3. Which large city in the southwest corner of Tennessee is on the Mississippi River?

4. Which river runs along Tennessee's western border?

5. Which large city in eastern Tennessee is at the intersections of Interstates 75 and 40?

6. Which river flows through Nashville?

7. Which city near the southern border is on the Tennessee River?

8. Which wildlife refuge is located in the northwest corner of the state?

9. Which popular hiking trail runs through the eastern side of Tennessee?

10. Which lake is north of Cleveland and south of Dayton?

Tennessee River

Pigeon Forge

10. Chickamauga Lake
9. The Appalachian Trail
8. The Reelfoot National Wildlife Refuge
7. Chattanooga
6. The Cumberland River
5. Knoxville
4. The Mississippi River
3. Memphis
2. The Great Smoky Mountains National Park
1. Nashville

State Flag, Seal, and Song

Tennessee's state flag, officially adopted in 1905, has a red background with a blue border on the right. Next to the border is a thin black band. In the middle of the red field is a blue circle with a thin white border. There are three stars inside the blue circle. They represent the state's three regions, or "grand divisions"—East Tennessee, Middle Tennessee, and West Tennessee.

Tennessee's state seal is divided into two halves. The top half shows images of a plow, a sheaf of wheat, and a cotton plant with the word Agriculture written below them. The bottom half has a picture of a riverboat, with the word Commerce below it. The border around the seal reads, "The Great Seal of the State of Tennessee." At the bottom is "1796"—the year Tennessee became a state.

For a state associated with music, it's not surprising that Tennessee should list ten state songs on its state website. The first to be adopted, in 1925, was "My Homeland, Tennessee." The lyrics are by Nell Grayson Taylor, and the music by Roy Lamont Smith. "Rocky Top" was added to the list in 1982, years after fans at University of Tennessee football games began singing it to support their Volunteers. It was written in 1967 by Felice and Boudleaux Bryant and recorded by the Osborne Brothers. To view the list and the lyrics for each song, visit **www.tn.gov/state-songs.shtml**

Glossary

civil rights   The fundamental rights guaranteed to all members of a society.

dam   A barrier holding back water, with the collected water used for a water supply or hydroelectric power.

ecosystem   The community of plants, animals, and other organisms interacting with their environment.

feral   An animal or other organism that was formerly captive or domestic, but has returned to a wild state.

fertile   Capable of producing life or offspring; in reference to land, a place which can produce bountiful crops.

Great Depression   The period from 1929 through most of the 1930s when the US and global economies weakened and many people were unable to find a job.

hydroelectric   Using the energy generated by flowing water to produce electricity.

limestone   A sedimentary rock often used for cement and building, made mostly of the skeletons of tiny marine creatures.

memorabilia   Things preserved for their historical significance, especially those connected with famous or important people.

panoramic   A wide view, encompassing the entire surroundings or landscape.

plantation   An estate on which crops are tended by people who live on the estate; especially used to refer to a large farm worked by slave labor.

Reconstruction   The period after the Civil War when the former Confederate states were brought back to the Union.

slavery   The condition of being the property of another person and being forced to work against your will.

sue   To take up legal action against someone.

volunteer   To freely take part in something without being forced or compelled.

More About Tennessee

BOOKS

Bobrick, Benson. *The Battle of Nashville*. New York: Knopf Books for Young Readers, 2010.

Gunderson, Megan M., *Andrew Johnson: Seventeenth President of the United States*. Minneapolis: ABDO Publishing, 2009.

Hasday, Judy L. *Davy Crockett*. Legends of the Wild West. New York: Chelsea House, 2010.

Marsico, Katie. *Andrew Jackson*. Presidents and Their Times. New York: Benchmark Books, 2010.

WEBSITES

Official Website of the State of Tennessee

www.tn.gov

Tennessee History for Kids!

www.tnhistoryforkids.org

Tennessee Travel and Tourism

www.tnvacation.com

ABOUT THE AUTHORS

William McGeveran is a former editorial director at World Almanac Books who now works as a freelance writer and editor.

Rick Petreycik has written articles on history, music, film, and business for publications such as *American Legacy*, *Rolling Stone*, *Disney Magazine*, *Yankee*, and the *Hartford Courant*. He lives in Connecticut with his wife, Pattilee.

Laura L. Sullivan is the author of many fiction and nonfiction books for children, including *Under the Green Hill* and *Love by the Morning Star*.

Index

Page numbers in **boldface** are illustrations. Entries in **boldface** are glossary terms.

African Americans, 33, 37–38, 41–42, 46–47, 50, 53, 71

agriculture, 27, 60, 65, 68, 76
See also farming

American Revolution, 28–29, 34

animals, *See* wildlife

Appalachian
Mountains, 7, 17–18, 29, 34, 45
Valley, 9, 12

Asian Americans, 47, 50, 53

birds, 4, 18–19

capital, *See* Kingston; Knoxville; Nashville

Chattanooga,12, 14–15, 34, 39, 51, 55, 67, 72, 75

Cherokee, 8, 24, 26–29, 31, 43, 49–50

Chickasaw, 24, 26, 31, 43

cities, *See* Chattanooga; Knoxville; Memphis; Nashville

civil rights, 15, 39, 42–43

Civil War, 31–33, 36, 43, 46, 72

climate, 16–17, 23, 50

Confederate, 32–33, 36–38, 47

cotton, 13, 16, 32, 36, 39–40, 65–66, 68, 73

counties, 7, 21, 29, 57

Creek (Native Americans), 24, 26, 50

Crockett, Davy, 28, 58, **62**, 62, 72

dam, 17, 41, 65, 68

economy, 31, 41–42, 51, 65, 67, 69, 71

ecosystem, 18

education, 51, 71

factories, 39–40, 65, 67, 71

farming, 12–13, 26, 31–32, 38, 40–41, 51, 65–66, 68, 71

feral, 19

fertile, 9, 13, 18, 45, 66

French and Indian War, 25, 43, 45,

government, 29, 31, 37, 41, 50, 57–61

governor, 29, 36, 59–61

Great Britain, 16, 25, 29, 43

Great Depression, 40

Hispanic Americans, 50–51, 53

hydroelectric, 41, 68

Jackson, Andrew, 31, 32, 35, 72

Johnson, Andrew, 33, 36–37, **36**, 72

King, Martin Luther Jr., 15, 42–43

Knoxville, 9, 29, 31, 34, **34**, 39, 43, 51, 54

limestone, 12, 20, 66, 69, 73

Lincoln, Abraham, 32–33, 36, 47

Index

manufacturing, 16, 39, 42, 65–69

memorabilia, 47

Memphis, 7, 14–17, 31, 34, **34**, 36, 39, 42–43, 47–49, 51, 53–54, 60, 71–72

mining, 39, 65–66, 69

mountains,
  Appalachians 8, 18, 29, 34
  Blue Ridge, 8
  Great Smoky, 8–9, **8**, **15**, 72
  Lookout, 15, 72
  Unaka, 8

Nashville, 12–14, 16–18, 25, 28–34, 39, 42, 47, 51, 53–55, 58, 69, 71–72, 75

Native Americans, 16, 24–27, 29, 31, 50, 53–54, 62
  See Cherokee, Creek, Chickasaw

New Deal programs, 41

panoramic, 9

plantation, 14, 32, 35

population, 45–47, 50

Reconstruction, 36–37

rivers,
  Cumberland, 13, **16**, 17, 28, 34, 36, 75
  Duck, 13
  Mississippi, 7, 9, 13, 15–16, 25, 29, 31, 34, 43, 45, 66, 75

Tennessee, **6**, 9, 13, 36, 41, 65, 75

settlers, 25–26, 28–29, 31–32, 45–47

Sevier, John, 29, **29**

slavery, 31–32, 37

soybeans, **13**, 65–66, 68

sue, 63

tornadoes, 17–18, 43

volunteer, 16, 29, 33

War of 1812, 16, 31, 35

World Wars I and II, 40–41